THE PAPERS OF MAJOR-GEN. NATHANAEL GREENE.

The recent effort on the part of the Historical Society to have a portion of the papers of Major-General Greene secured to the State of his nativity, has given rise to the thought that an account of the manuscripts left by him may be of interest to the readers of the society's publications.

General Greene preserved his papers with great care. One reason was, that his intimate friend, President Joseph Reed of Pennsylvania, formerly adjutant-general to General Washington, contemplating a history of the Revolutionary War, asked General Greene to preserve for him everything that could be of assistance to him in that project. The general did so. There is also evidence that he intended to publish some account of his own military career. In a letter to John Adams, dated January 28, 1781, he says: "The American armies have gained some advantage; my public letters will have given you some idea of them, but the previous measures which led to important events, and my reasons for those measures, must lie in the dark until a more leisure hour."* The papers which he preserved were consulted by two contemporary historians of the Revolution, Gordon and Ramsay, though Reed did not live to carry out his design. Gordon consulted them at Newport, and afterward addressed many inquiries to General Greene, which were evidently to be answered by means of these papers.† Ramsay took notes from General Greene's manuscripts.‡ The papers which Greene retained

*Johnson's Greene, Vol. I., pp. v., vi.

†Letters of Gordon, in Greene's Greene, Vol. II., pp. 417, 418; and in Hist. Magazine, Vol. XIII, pp. 24, 25.

‡Letter of Ramsay in Hist. Magazine, Vol. XIII., p. 26.

in his own hands were those of his private correspondence, as distinguished from the official papers of the Southern Department during the period while he was in command. The letters were, at the disbanding of the Continental Army, entrusted to the care of Major Edward Rutledge. On his death they passed into the hands of his son, Henry Rutledge. When Henry Rutledge left South Carolina to live in Tennessee, he left these papers in the charge of General Charles Cotesworth Pinckney of Charleston.*

General Greene, dying in Georgia in 1786, left a widow and five children. His widow married Phinehas Miller, and died in 1814. His eldest son, George Washington Greene, died unmarried in 1794. His eldest daughter, Martha Washington Greene, married first John C. Nightingale, and afterward Dr. Henry Turner, with whom she lived in Tennessee. The second daughter, Cornelia Lott, married first Peyton Skipwith, and afterward Edward B. Littlefield, and also went to live in Tennessee. The next child, a son, Nathanael Ray Greene, lived in East Greenwich, Rhode Island. The youngest daughter, Louisa Catherine, a posthumous child, married James Shaw and lived on Cumberland Island, Georgia. When Justice William Johnson, of the Supreme Court of the United States, began to occupy himself with the life of General Greene, the private papers of the general were in the possession of this youngest daughter, Mrs. Shaw.†

"Some years since," says Justice Johnson in the preface to his 'Sketches of General Greene,' "I was consulted by Mrs. Shaw, the youngest daughter and administratrix of General Greene, on the manner in which she should dispose of her father's original papers. Until that time I had never understood that they had been preserved. For the first time I learnt that they had been carefully husbanded, and never yet submitted to the examination of any one, with a view either to add to the materials of general history or furnish those of a biography of the great man who had bequeathed them to posterity. Nor had I, until then, been struck with the fact that

*Johnson, Vol. I., p. v.

†Johnson, Vol. II., pp. 462, 463.

his biography had never been attempted, nor his name even mentioned in the cyclopædias of the day. I therefore suggested to Mrs. Shaw that, if she approved of my undertaking the biography of her father, I would take the papers under my care, and examine how far they afforded the necessary materials for such an undertaking. The proposal was readily assented to, and she soon after forwarded to me a large collection of letters containing his private correspondence ; and addressed a letter to Gen. Charles Cotesworth Pinckney, requesting him to deliver me the trunk containing the official papers of the Southern Department, whilst General Greene was in command. The latter were immediately delivered up to me, and I found them in the highest state of preservation and arrangement. . . . . These two collections of papers, consisting of several thousand, had obviously been preserved with great care, and the motive became explained in the course of examining them."*

Incidentally, Judge Johnson mentions that all Greene's letters were written by himself, so that these collections of papers were a collection of autographic memorials of him.†

Beside these papers derived from the descendants of his hero, the biographer describes other manuscript materials for his work. In 1818 he visited Rhode Island, and during the summer explored the private cabinets of the general's friends in the northern and eastern States.‡ "I found," he says, "that the general's early correspondence had been religiously preserved, and that various small collections of historical materials had been made, which were now liberally communicated to me, to aid in a work in the promotion of which every one manifested an individual interest." He mentions such obligations to Governor Gibbs of Rhode Island; his brother, Colonel Gibbs of Long Island; the surviving brothers and nephews of General Greene ; his early friends, Colonel Ward and General Varnum ; Judge Pendleton of New York, who had made

*Johnson, Vol. I., p. v.

†Johnson, Vol. II., p. 458.

‡Johnson, Vol. I.. pp. vi.–ix.

preparation for writing a biography;* Joseph Reed; the relatives of Colonel Petit; the widow of General Harmar; the sons of Col. Otho Williams; Gen. C. C. Pinckney and Gen. W. R. Davie. He declares that he had "a mass of four thousand original letters, written by the hands of all the distinguished men" of the period, and that, among them, the select letters of Washington, Lafayette, Steuben, Read and Greene, beside those which he published, would alone make up two interesting volumes.

At Philadelphia, Justice Johnson was offered by Desilver, the publisher, a mass of original materials regarding Greene, from which a biography was at that time being made for Desilver. A thousand dollars was asked, and the judge refused. He declares that they were only the vouchers of the quartermaster-general's department; and adds, "If ever that collection of papers has furnished, or shall furnish, to the world, one page of history or biography (unless it be a *fac-simile* page), I shall acknowledge my error in not possessing myself of them." This last is a most direct thrust at the "Memoirs of the Life and Campaigns of Nathaniel Greene," by Charles Caldwell, M. D., Professor of Natural History in the University of Pennsylvania, which Desilver published in 1819. Caldwell's book contained little that had not already been printed in Gen. Henry Lee's "Memoirs of the War in the Southern Department;" but it did contain, as a frontispiece, a *fac-simile* of a letter of Greene. Dr. Caldwell declares in his preface that "the documents and other sources from which we have derived our information are as ample and authentic as any now existing;" but that this was very far from being the case is evident from the pages of Justice Johnson's book, as well as from his preface.

Johnson's two ponderous tomes were published in 1822. From this time one hears nothing more of the papers which had been committed to his charge until more than forty years later. During that time they had passed from the custody of Mrs. Shaw, the general's youngest daughter, into that of Mr. Phinehas Miller Nightingale, second son of the eldest

*Ramsay used a manuscript of Pendleton's, written before 1782. See his letter in Hist. Magazine, Vol. XIII., p. 26.

daughter. In 1846, George Washington Greene, the general's grandson, published a short life of his grandfather in Sparks's "Library of American Biography," of which it constituted the twentieth volume. But that book was written at Rome, remote from the manuscript sources for a complete biography. In its preface the author expressed a hope of being able later to use those materials in the preparation of an ampler work. In 1866, he used a portion of them in preparing the pamphlet called "An examination of some statements concerning Major-Gen. Greene, in the ninth volume of Bancroft's History." In the preface to the elaborate life which he published in 1867 and in 1871, he says that on his return to the United States the Greene papers were entrusted to him by Mr. Nightingale, and that they formed a collection of over six thousand documents. While in his possession at East Greenwich they were at times seen by members of the Rhode Island Historical Society, and an effort was made by Professor Greene, assisted by Charles Sumner, Charles Butler, and James S. Thayer, to have them purchased and printed by the government of the United States. They subsequently returned to the custody of the heirs in Georgia, and were, till lately, in the hands of Mrs. P. M. Nightingale of Brunswick, Georgia. In the winter of 1893–94 an effort was made by a committee of the Rhode Island Historical Society to secure their purchase by the State. In furtherance of this project, a member of the family in Georgia drew up from the papers a list or rather an enumeration of the letters composing the mass of manuscripts, which was forwarded to a member of the committee. It showed some 1,900 letters from General Greene, and nearly 2,500 letters written to him. The former were written to a large variety of correspondents, especially concerning the war in the Southern States. The latter included fifty-five letters from General Washington, forty-seven from Congress and the Board of War, forty-six from Lafayette, 116 from General Marion, 114 from Col. Henry Lee, sixty-seven from Colonel Laurens, sixty-three from Colonel Carrington, fifty-seven from Colonel Wadsworth, fifty-seven from General Sumter, forty-seven from Gen. Anthony Wayne, forty-three from Gen. Otho

Williams, thirty-four from General Steuben, twenty-seven from General Lincoln, twenty-six from General Kosciuszko, and lesser numbers from other Revolutionary commanders,—General Weeden, General Pickens, General Varnum, General Gist, General Knox, Gen. Wade Hampton, General St. Clair, Count d'Estaing, Count Rochambeau, thirty-seven from Captain Hamilton,—and on the other side, for instance, thirteen from Howe and one from Cornwallis. More than two hundred letters from governors of the various States were embraced, including some from Governors Greene and Collins of Rhode Island, Dickinson and Read of Pennsylvania and Delaware, Jefferson and Harrison of Virginia, and larger numbers from Rutledge and other governors of southern States. One may also mention thirty-four letters to General Greene from Robert Morris, six from Gouverneur Morris, five from Richard Henry Lee, and seven from the Minister of France.

Rich as this collection was, it was found that the State of Rhode Island could certainly not be induced to pay the price asked by the present representatives of General Greene, and the whole mass of Greene MSS. was, it is understood, sold to a dealer in autographs in New York City.

It may be interesting if some information is added respecting other papers and letters of General Greene than those which are in the hands of his descendants. In the library of the Department of State at Washington there are two volumes of his letters, extending from July 8, 1776, to August 22, 1785; two volumes of transcripts of his letters from October 27, 1780, to November 3, 1783; and five volumes of his letters and papers relative to the department of the quartermaster-general in 1779 and 1780.* In the library of Congress there are letter-books of 1781 and 1782, two volumes.† Caldwell, in his preface to the work already mentioned, says: "No inconsiderable portion of the materials necessary to complete his biography have been lost through the negligence of those to whom they were entrusted. In various parts of the coun-

*Bulletin of the Bureau of Rolls and Library, Vol. I., pp. 19, 20.

†Winsor, Narrative and Critical History, Vol. VIII., p. 413; Bancroft, Vol. X., p. 7.

try, individuals are known to have been in possession of volumes of his official letters, some of which no doubt contained interesting information on the subject of his campaigns. But, on the strictest inquiry, few of these documents are now to be found." In view of Caldwell's relations to Desilver, and Desilver's relations to Johnson, this has an amusing sound. But that Johnson also had not exhausted the material, was asserted with much warmth of feeling by Henry Lee, son of Gen Henry Lee ("Light-horse Harry"), in his book published in 1824, entitled, "The Campaign of 1781 in the Carolinas; with Remarks Historical and Critical on Johnson's Life of Greene." The book consists of a series of most bitter comments on Johnson, who had minimized the importance of General Lee's services and the degree of his intimacy with General Greene and of Greene's reliance upon him. Johnson had said, "The cabinets of all his most intimate friends have been open to us, and to us alone." Commenting on this, the younger Lee says: "We have the best authority for affirming that about five years ago, Mr. Edmund I. Lee, of Alexandria, made application in behalf of Judge Johnson to one of the representatives of the late General Lee for the inspection of his military papers, and for the use of such as might have reference to the life of General Greene. That in reply Mr. Lee was assured there were a number of letters from General Greene among those papers, which were illustrative and characteristic, although there was no sketch of his life. That the originals would not be given up, but that Judge Johnson was welcome to copies. Nothing further was heard on the subject, and it is natural to inquire for what cause Judge Johnson, who appears to have traversed the continent, and even to have disinterred the heroic dead in search of materials, should have forborne to have availed himself of the opportunity of inspecting General Greene's correspondence with an officer who is acknowledged to have exhibited 'brilliant military talents,' and a 'cordial and devoted attachment to his general.'"* Lee gives several letters which Johnson had declared

*Lee, p. 11.

to be missing "from the official files," and says that Johnson "acknowledges more than one *hiatus* in his copies of General Greene's letters to Lee." Greene and Lee, by the way, conducted a part of their correspondence in cipher.*

Sparks collected many letters of Greene. In his diary, in a passage published by Dr. Adams,† he says, under date of May 15, 1826, writing at Richmond after searches in the State capitol, "Many letters from Greene are on the files which I have looked over to-day,—some of them written in a vigorous strain, and indicating not more a great commander than a man of high intellectual power and knowledge of mankind. I marked several to be copied." Again, in a passage not printed, he says, under date of June 7, 1827, at New York: "Mr. Ward informed me of papers in his father's possession, particularly letters from General Greene. His father is the son of Governor Ward of Rhode Island, and holds his papers. Mr. Ward mentioned particularly a eulogy on General Greene by Hamilton, pronounced before the Cincinnati Society. It was never published. Mr. Ward had procured a copy for Mrs. Shaw, General Greene's daughter." Next day, June 8, "Mr. Ward has in his possession several letters from General Greene, written in early life, which I am to consult hereafter." At a later date he writes, October 12, 1827, Boston: "Returned this day from a visit to Providence, to which place I have been for the purpose of consulting Mrs. Shaw, the daughter of General Greene, respecting her father's papers. These belong to Mrs. Shaw. They are now in the possession of Judge Johnson, who has had them for the purpose of writing his Life of General Greene. On Mrs. Shaw's return to Charleston, she says she shall reclaim the papers, and she manifests the best disposition to afford me every facility in consulting them. She will come again to Providence in the summer, and she will then probably bring the papers with her, and allow me to retain them while I am engaged in preparing Washington's Works." At Philadelphia, under

*Lee, pp. 232, 12, 324, 325.

†Adams's Sparks, Vol. II., p. 457.

date of February 4, 1831, he notes that there are in the library of the American Philosophical Society twelve volumes of Greene's manuscripts, covering a period of a year and a half. They were in the main simply the papers of the quartermaster-general's department, and seemed to him to contain little of value, though after examination he selected a certain number to be copied. No doubt these were the papers which in 1818 were in the possession of Desilver.*

A considerable number of letters and copies of letters of General Greene are among the Sparks MSS. in the library of Harvard University; others among the Steuben papers in the library of the New York Historical Society, and in other repositories of Revolutionary correspondence. Peter Force collected a number. The Rhode Island Historical Society printed some letters of Greene in the volume called "Revolutionary Correspondence from 1775 to 1782," which formed Vol. VI. of their collections. There are some among the papers of Gen. Peter Horry of South Carolina (Winsor, VIII. 458), and one or two have been printed from the manuscripts possessed by Nathaniel Paine of Worcester and George Brinley. (Hist. Magazine, Vol. XI., pp. 98, 204).

J. FRANKLIN JAMESON.

*MS. diary of President Sparks.

NOTES ON LANDSCAPES IN THE PICTURE GALLERY.

NOTES ON LANDSCAPES IN THE PICTURE GALLERY.

A notice of some of the landscapes in the picture gallery was given in the librarian's report for 1892, and may be found in Vol. I. of the quarterly publication, on pages from 66 to 71. The landscapes in the picture gallery are as attractive to a large class of visitors as the portraits, and undoubtedly serve an important purpose in perpetuating a correct knowledge of our local history. For these reasons, and to obviate the need of personal explanations, these notes are furnished, together with two admirably engraved illustrations. All of the landscapes belong to the present century, while several of the portraits date far back in the last century.

I. THE OLD DROP SCENE.

The largest and the oldest landscape in this cabinet, and perhaps the largest in this State, is 21 x 23 feet, and occupies the wall of the north end of the auditorium. This picture was the drop scene of the old Providence Theatre, and represents a part of the east side of Providence as it was eighty-three years ago. When the picture was taken it was regarded as a great enterprise, and its exhibition proved a great attraction at the theatre for a long period. It was painted between 1808 and 1812, by John Worrall, a noted scene-painter of Boston. It was first exhibited on the 8th of July, 1812. It was purchased by a committee of this society consisting of William E. Richmond and Thomas F. Carpenter in 1832, when the theatre became the property of the corporation of Grace Church. This is the earliest picture, though not the best one, of the cove in the possession of the society, and it is the only one in which trees constitute an important part of the scenery.

www.ingramcontent.com/pod-product-compliance
Lightning Source LLC
LaVergne TN
LVHW010317160826
845475LV00009B/2182